Algiers - The Untold Story

The African American Experience
1929 - 1955

Written by:

Allyson Ward Neal

Contributors:

Alvin Aubry, Ph.D.
Gloria Bailey
Moses Bailey
Emma Harper Bryant
Tyrone Casby, Sr.
Donald E. DeVore, Ph.D.
Erma Gibbs
Dorothy Brown Johnson
Martha B. Mallory
Elizabeth Pierce
Minerva Victor Simmons
Herbert H. Simpson
John Spencer
Deborah Stewart
Lillian Alveris Williams
James R. Williams
Lula Mae B. Ward

MW00427709

Publication of this book was made possible by
a grant from the:
Louisiana Endowment for the Humanities

Sponsored by:
Beautiful Zion Baptist Church
Reverend James R. Williams, Pastor

Library of Congress Catalog Number: 2001118854
ISBN Number: 0-9714320-0-7

Copyright © 2001
Beautiful Zion Baptist Church
1017 Elmira Avenue
New Orleans, Louisiana 70114

Published by:
Beautiful Zion Baptist Church

Contents

Dedicated to those who have lived, loved and overcome. May God continue to bless and keep you.

Acknowledgements

"We will be so careful to give you all the glory, honor and praise ... thank you God for divine inspiration."

All of the untold stories of African Americans living in Algiers between 1929 and 1955 could not be contained in the modest pages of this publication. However, the stories that have been told provide insight into the lives of a people that are often overlooked and forgotten.

The stories and recollections would not have been transformed into this volume without the support, assistance and cooperation of members of the Algiers Community. To those that lent their stories, memories and photographs: thank you.

Those persons include Alvin Aubry, Ph.D., Gloria Bailey, Moses Bailey, Emma Harper Bryant, Tyrone Casby, Sr., Erma Gibbs, Dorothy Brown Johnson, Martha B. Mallory, Elizabeth Pierce, Minerva Victor Simmons, Herbert H. Simpson, John Spencer, Deborah Stewart, Lillian Alveris Williams, James R. Williams and Lula Mae B. Ward.

Thank you to Jane Palmer, Branch Manager at the Algiers Point Library for the assistance and encouragement that you provided during the early stages of the project. Thank you to Dr. Donald E. DeVore, history professor, for readily agreeing to lend your expertise to this endeavor, and thanks also to Kalamu Ya Salam, renown poet, for joining the team as well.

Appreciation must be expressed to Jennifer Mitchel, Assistant Director of the Louisiana Endowment for the Humanities, for encouraging us to pursue the grant that funded this project. Thank you for your advice, time and patience.

Thanks to all the members of Beautiful Zion Baptist Church for your support and encouragement. Thank you to the staff at the Amistad Research Center for your advice, assitance and guidance.

This publication is merely the beginning and is meant to serve as a launching pad for future books highlighting the lives of African Americans living in Algiers. The history contained in the community is rich, awe-inspiring and deserves to be told. Younger generations must know from whence they have come in order to appreciate what they have and to know where they are going. We hope this book inspires others to search deeper.

Introduction

Just as threads are delicately woven to create fabric, so are the lives of individuals tied together by common experiences to form a community. The story of African Americans living in Algiers, a small community on the Westbank of the Mississippi River in New Orleans, is a story that has yet to be told.

For many, the journey began in Africa, it took a turn for the worse during the Middle Passage and tragically ended on the auction block in the historic Congo Square of New Orleans.

Slavery, with all of its ills and travesties against humanity, remains the most common experience that binds all African Americans in the United States. In Algiers, slavery tied many African Americans together and still do until this day.

This story is based on oral interviews that examine the experiences of African Americans who lived in Algiers between 1929 and 1955. Aspects of those experiences include the social values, culture and faith of a people who were relegated to living in servitude to a large society. Their stories are so compelling that readers will be allowed to look back into the past and share their pain, difficulties, triumphs and tragedies.

Algiers Map

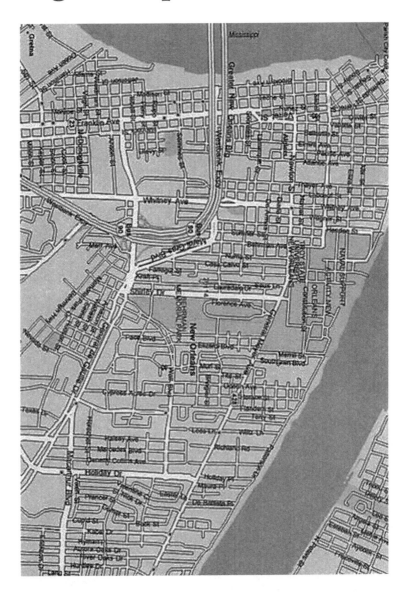

Algiers History

With its beginnings in the 1700s, Algiers was a rich, yet undeveloped land that contained plantations. Additionally, because New Orleans is a port City, the slave trade was an important aspect of commerce for this growing province.

Jean Baptiste Le Moyne Bienville established New Orleans in 1718. However, it is fitting to note that a few thousand Choctaw Indians lived in and traveled throughout the region for many years before French explorers arrived.

After establishing or "discovering" New Orleans, Bienville was granted the West Bank portion of the Mississippi River and part of this area later became known as Algiers.

From 1718 until the late 1800s, Algiers experienced several transformations that included the sale of property, railroad developments, French and Indain wars, the transition from French to Spanish rule and even the Battle of New Orleans.

For many years the community governed itself independently of the City of New Orleans under the jurisdiction of a police jury. In 1870, Algiers was annexed to the City of New Orleans and became its Fifth Municipal District.

The Duverje family is the first family of the area and occupied a plantation house (where the old Algiers Courthouse stands) that was constructed in 1812. In addition to the Duverje family, Algiers was home to several other wealthy families, some of whom have been immortalized by the small communities within Algiers that have been named for them.

Those communities include, but are not limited to, McDonoghville, Aurora, Oakdale, Belleville, Leesville and others. Streets also bear the names of Algiers' leading families including Verret, Vallette, Olivier, Delaronde and Lavergne. Additionally, the leading ladies or "Southern Belles" of those families were honored with street names such as Elmira, Evelina, Eliza and Alix.

Many African Americans who are native to Algiers and who can re-trace their roots for more than three generations will find that their ancestors lived and worked on the plantations that fueled this small town's economy.

In addition, some may have been free men and women of color. According to Donald McNabb and Lee Madere's *A History of New Orleans*, by 1803, there fewer than 5,000 African-Americans in New Orleans with more free men of color than slaves.

They found that only 8% of the population, or one out of every twelve persons in the city, were slaves. Additionally, most slaves were not used for manual labor, but were mainly household servants. In 1850, it was reported that slaves comprised 16% of the population.

The percentage of slaves relative to the entire population reflected the increasingly high demand and price of slaves for plantation work.

Slaves often learned skills and hired themselves out for additional work and paid their owners a commission on their earnings. Many individual slaves bought their freedom this way and further reduced the slave population. In 1860, there were only two families in New Orleans that owned in excess of 100 slaves. The remaining 4,162 slave-holders each kept an average of three slaves. Free persons of color comprised six percent of New Orleans' population in the 1800s. Some were freed slaves or their offspring were free persons of color.

Most often, free persons of color spoke French, were Catholic, and generally favored French culture. Many free persons of color were small businessmen and artisans who played an important role in New Orleans' economic development.

Untold Stories

The personal stories that have been told recounting the experiences of the slaves and those fortunate enough to be free persons of color, still remain in the hearts of African American residents in the Algiers community.

The stories have helped shape the lives of those who experienced the tumultuous time through the eyes and ears of their grandparents. They are stories that have been left undocumented, yet they exist. They are stories that are not widely discussed, yet they are passed on from generation to generation.

Though many prominent residents grace the pages of the few history books about this small and quaint community, the African Americans who lived, but were left out of the pages are also a part of the great richness that is Algiers. They too, are Algiers. They are, Algiers: the untold story.

Chapter One
The Depression Years

In the late 1920s, many years after African Americans first began their lives in Algiers as slaves, the social values, the culture and the faith instilled in them were still being taught, practiced and passed on to their descendants.

In 1929, the nation experienced what has been called one of the most devastating eras in the history of the United States. The Great Depression, as it is known, was a period of darkness for most Americans. When the stock market crashed in October of 1929, the country took its first step toward staggering unemployment, poverty, homelessness and utter despair.

In 1930, 31,444 people were unemployed in Louisiana and 2,598,151 were unemployed in the United States. The New Orleans Times Picayune reported on collapsing banks, and occurrences of men performing daunting acts out of frustration after losing money, jobs and homes.

However, the Depression experienced by the average American was not the same Depression experienced by African Americans living in Algiers. These citizens never shared in the prosperity and wealth of the roaring 1920s.

Furthermore, poverty had remained a constant factor within the African American community in Algiers since slavery. Therefore, the old adage "nothing ventured, nothing gained" aptly described the conditions for African American Algierines during the Great Depression. Those that grew up in Algiers during the Depression recalled a time where life as they knew it was never interrupted.

Lillian Alveris Williams
Retired Nurse

Lilliam Alveris Williams at a church extravaganza hosted by Beautiful Zion Baptist Church, 1017 Elmira Avenue, in the 1930s.

Lillian Alveris Williams, who grew up in a single-parent family, was seventeen-years-old when the stock market crashed, but remembered that African Americans in Algiers seemed to be left untouched by the turn of events. "We had a nice life at that time... We didn't have too much, but we lived beautifully with what we had," she said.

Her mother, Rosie Alveris, worked as a domestic. She had one brother, Rayfield, who is deceased and has one sister, Buelah, who now lives on the Eastbank of New Orleans.

The Alveris family lived on Homer Street in a predominantly white neighborhood. Williams recalls that during her youth, all of her neighbors worked and no one appeared to be in dire straits during the Depression.

She attended McDonogh #32 Elementary School, a public school for African Americans. For her high school education, she attend Xavier Prepatory School, a private school for African Americans. Williams remembered that tuition for Xavier Prep, as it is known, was $5 per month.

The family attended church at Mount Pilgrim Fourth Baptist Church at 429 Newton Street in Algiers. Williams sometimes attended Sunday School at St. Mathew United Methodist Church at 1100 Verret Street. She joined Beautiful Zion Baptist Church, at 1017 Elmira Avenue, in 1934 where the Reverend G. C. Rounds served as Pastor. Later, she married Edwin C. Williams, now deceased, and both attended Beautiful Zion.

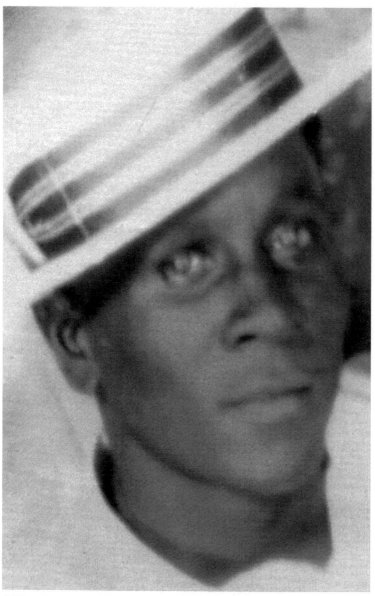

Lillian Alveris Williams' husband, Edwin C. Williams is pictured here sometime in the 1930s.

Lillian Alveris Williams' youngest son, James R. Williams graduated from L.B. Landry High School in 1960.

Lillian Alveris Williams is pictured here with her son, Roland Williams at his ninth-grade promotion ceremony at L.B. Landry High School in 1943.

A photo from the Williams family album shows L.B. Landry High School's Homecoming Queen and Court in the 1950s.

New Orleans' economy was tied to its location near the outlet of the greatest river in the United States, the Mississippi River. The shipping docks or dry docks, and the railroad were major sources of industry in New Orleans that provided jobs for Algiers residents. Many people held jobs at the Southern Pacific Railroad located in Algiers including Williams' husband, Edwin. Prior to working for the "SP", as it was commonly known, Edwin, worked for Manual Lombard's coal, ice and wood shop. Lombard, an Afircan American, was known throughout Algiers for providing jobs and supporting local sports and civic activities.

Williams recalled that the social life in Algiers was reserved to dances and church activities. Dances were sometimes held at the Elks or Odd Fellows Hall on Elmira and Lamarque Streets where the "dip" and the "jitterbug" were the popular dances.

Live bands played at the dances and the renowned Jazz veteran "Kid" Thomas Valentine, who is deceased, often led musical renditions with his Algiers Stompers band. Williams remembered attending dances with her boyfriend who later became her husband.

"We would be dancing up a storm. He would follow me to the ladies room and wait outside for me to come out. And all the other guys would complain and say, 'Aw man, you don't give nobody else a chance to dance with her,'" she said.

Other social outlets consisted of attending the movies at the Folly Theatre on Teche Street. Jim Crow laws prevented African Americans from enjoying many benefits that White citizens of Algiers enjoyed. The community's public areas were segregated, however race relations were reported to be good and usually free of overt hostility.

Williams remembered sitting on the back of the streetcar behind a screen for many years. She also said that African Americans could not cross Opelousas Street unless they were working as domestics in the area.

There were laws to enforce segregation and unwritten rules that the races seemed to abide by making life pleasant and undisturbed for the affluent. And although African Americans knew that they were treated unfairly, life continued and race relations were amicable.

Beautiful Zion Baptist Church, where Williams is a member, held many social functions and special events. This extravaganza was held in the 1930s.

The churches in the African American community played a large role in shaping attitudes and moral convictions, which may have helped the races to live harmoniously, though amidst occasional violence. "Faith played a big part," Williams said, "That was our weapon and it still is because God is still on the throne."

One incident that tragically altered Williams' life was the murder of her husband Edwin in 1946. As he walked to Beautiful Zion Baptist Church one evening to meet his wife after choir rehearsal, Edwin Williams was beaten to death by a group of white servicemen. African Americans in Algiers were outraged by the murder and still speak of it today.

The men were not natives of Algiers, but were brought to the community via the United States Navy and were stationed at the Algiers Naval Base. The men were never charged for the murder.

The Williams Singers are shown here with their music instructor. Two of Lillian Alveris Williams' sons, Joe Williams (front row, second from left) and Edwin Williams (front row, right), were members of the group.

Lillian Alveris Williams' nieces, pictured at left and right: Evelina Alveris and Joyce Alveris, pose for wedding party photographs in the 1940s.

Elizabeth Pierce

Retired Domestic Worker

Elizabeth Pierce, born in 1912, was also seventeen-years-old during the Depression. Pierce's family moved from Thibodeaux, Louisiana to Algiers when she was six-years-old and lived at 222 Socrates Street.

She said her family left Thibodeaux during the influenza epidemic of 1918 and because of the scarcity of jobs. "People were dying and work was scarce. The influenza epidemic was so bad that people couldn't receive a proper burial. They just put them in pine boxes and buried them," she recalled.

Pierce lost three sisters to the epidemic, Stella, Edna and Verna. She and her younger sister Priscilla were the only two to survive.

Upon relocating to Algiers, Pierce's mother worked as a domestic and her father worked in the railroad industry. "Times were hard, but in the midst of it all, we made it," she said.

McDonogh #32 was the only elementary school available to African Americans and Pierce attended. At the age of ten-years-old, she began working part time as a domestic on weekends where she earned $1 per day.

Her family was poor and, at the time, her mother and father had separated. She had to work to assit her mother in the care of her sister Priscilla and sister Sylvia, who came later. Pierce never returned to school and worked various jobs that included cleaning offices at the Southern Pacific Railroad.

She remembered Algiers as a small community where neighbors were friendly and helpful. Economic conditions for African Americans were not great, but the kindness and care of other community members helped families to forge ahead. "The community was better then. We didn't have to worry about locking our doors. We could leave the house, pull the door closed, and when we returned, everything would still be in place," she said.

Pierce recalled that wages during the late 1920s and early 1930s were low. Earnings ranged from $3 to $3.50 per day. Food prices were also moderate and accommodated the wages people earned. Bread, pickled meat or ham, a half of a pound of red beans and a half of a pound of rice could all be purchased for a nickel each.

Fresh "springer" chickens and "stewing" hens could be purchased for 50 cents each. Rent ranged from $3 to $6 per month and some homes did not have electricity. Wood and coal burning stoves, kerosine lamps and fireplaces provided sources of heat and light. Cisterns were used to provide water for various uses and "out houses" or outside toilets were common in the Algiers community. Those who could afford homes with electricty, running water and in-door plumbing were considered fortunate.

"We didn't have a lot of money, but we had food on our table and clothes on our back. We were just poor people trying to make a living. They didn't pay much back then like they pay now. Sometimes you had to have two jobs to really make it," she said.

Domestic work was common among African American women in Algiers. "That was about all you could do unless you had a good education," said Pierce.

She also recalled that there were jobs at sewing factories, seafood factories and farms. Several women also provided domestic services from their own homes like washing and ironing clothes. Women were paid 50 cents for washing a load of laundry and 75 cents for ironing clothes. Since money was scarce during the Depression, spending was limited to the essential needs for living such as food, shelter and transportation.

Transporation sometimes was seen as a luxury as many Algierines who lived in the community during the Depression remember walking long distances to get to and from their jobs, homes, schools, stores, relatives homes and churches.

Public transportation in Algiers consisted of the streetcar and the ferry boat. The streetcar transported community members throughout the Algiers and Gretna communities with its most popular stop at the Algiers/Canal Street Ferry.

The cost to ride the street car was five cents. The Algiers/ Canal Street Ferry transported passengers from the Westbank of the Mississippi River to the Eastbank where the boat docked at the foot of the infamous Canal Street. The fare for the ferry boat was five cents and riders had to purchase tickets before boarding.

With money being allocated for the essentials only, shopping was secondary and sewing one's own clothes was primary as many women made clothes for themselves and their family members.

Pierce recalled her sewing experiences. "I learned how to sew at an early age and I made my own dress patterns. I drew my patterns using old newspapers.

"Sometimes I would buy a pattern for one penny or 15 cents. Then I would buy my material for about 15 cents per yard. I would make clothes for myself, my sisters and my mother," Pierce said.

Low wages and poor living conditions did not deter Pierce. She summed up her life experiences as being hard lessons that shaped her character. "I thank God for my life in the past because it taught me something.

"It was educational. It makes me more compassionate for others. There isn't a month that goes by that I don't reach out to somebody. I don't say much about it. I'm not the type to brag, but when I have the opportunity to reach out to someone else, I do, because I had it kind of rough coming up," she said, "I thank God for where I came from, because the Lord has blessed me... I'm 89 years old and I can do for myself. I take care of my own house and my business and that's a blessing."

Erma Henderson Gibbs

Semi-Retired Funeral Director

Erma Henderson Gibbs was the first African American woman in New Orleans to obtain a funeral director's license.

Erma Henderson Gibbs was 26-years-old in 1930 during the Great Depression, and part owner of the Murray Henderson Funeral Home of Algiers. The funeral home was established in 1910 when Gibbs was six-years-old.

Her father, Murray Henderson started the business with the help of his employers who operated the John A. Barrett Funeral Home. Henderson married Olivia Calvin and they had three children, Lillian, Erma and Delia who died at the age of six. The Hendersons lived on Lamarque Street in Algiers and later moved to 324 Diana Street where the funeral home was founded.

The family owned a four-room Creole cottage on Diana Street which had an office on the side where families could make funeral arrangements. In 1913, the funeral home was relocated to 1209-11 Teche Street where it remains today.

Murray Henderson died in 1930 at the age of 47. His wife, Olivia had died some years prior at the age of 45. After Henderson's death, his daughter, Erma assumed the responsibilities of operating the business along with her sister Lillian Henderson Dunn and cousin Charles Henderson.

Gibbs remembered the Depression as a time when community members were closely knit. Her family was self sufficient in that they owned their own business and used their gardens and farm animals as major sources of food supply.

"My family had gardens with fruit trees, and they also raised hogs. When they killed a hog, they would give parts of it to the neighbors. They would also pickle some of (the meat) for seasonings," she said, "And things were very cheap then. One dollar went a long way at the grocery store."

Gibbs recalled that neighbors were considerate of one another during the Depression. She admits that the circumstances were difficult and even more so for families who were not as fortunate as hers. "People cared about each other. They would visit your home or you would visit theirs. Their children would come into your house. People would look after the children in the neighborhod," she said.

During the Depression, funeral expenses were priced as low as $300, but for that time it was an enormous amount of money. Funerals were also performed differently than they are today as Gibbs pointed out. Many of the services were provided at the deceased person's home. "At that time, we didn't have a funeral home. We only had an office. Everything was done out of the person's house. The men would elbalm them and then put them on a cot with a velvet cover. The family would wake them that night. Then for the funeral they would put them in a casket, take them to the church and then to the cemetery to bury them," she said.

Gibbs' father was one of several African American business owners in Algiers who was known for his philanthropic efforts. He had a reputation for assisting poor families with costly funeral expenses.

"Poor people really didn't have the money (for funeral expenses) and my father helped them," she said. In Robert Meyer, Jr.'s *Names Over New Orleans Public Schools*,

Henderson is characterized as a kind man who was willing to help his fellow man.

Meyer wrote, "He seems to have had little interest in accumulating money, but he was keen to assist those who were less fortunate than himself. In doing so, he expressed his kindly way of life, his ideals and his benevolence in various ways. For example, at Christmastime, he is said to have provided toys for needy children and gifts for dependent oldsters. During the severe influenza epidemic of 1918, he is reported to have paid the medical expenses of many persons and to have provided food for impoverished convalescents. He worked steadily, but unobtrusively over many years to obtain recreational and other improvements for Algiers. Yet he sought no praise for his work."

After his death, Gibbs and her sister Lillian continued their father's good will by making financial contributions to neighborhood schools and churches. They also assisted students who aspired to obtain college degrees. Gibbs is 97-years-old and still shows concern for the Algiers community. Additionally, she supervises ten employees at the Henderson Undertaking Company and has received several awards and accolades for her commitment to others.

Of the Depression, Gibbs remembered that although some families were less fortunate than others, there was a deep concern for all and love thy neighbor was not only preached, but practiced. "We had our ups and downs, but we had some good times and the Lord was really good to us," she said, "Like the song says, 'I won't complain'."

Emma Harper Bryant
Retired Administrative Assistant

Emma Harper Bryant was born in 1927 and was only two years old at the onset of the Depression. She remembered standing in food and bread lines as a young girl. "We used to have to get commodities. I remember we had to stand in line on Elmira Street to get food. We also had to go to the Algiers Courthouse to get the milk," she said.

Bryant's family lived at 719 Newton Street. The household consisted of her immediate family: mother, father and siblings; and her grandparents who owned the home.

As some families in Algiers did not have the conveniences of indoor plumbing and electricity, Bryant's family was fortunate in that they enjoyed such luxuries.

"We were blessed. We lived with my grandfather. We had electricity and we even had a telephone. We weren't allowed to use the telephone. None of our friends had telephones so we didn't really have anyone to talk to. We were exposed to a lot. We had a dining room and we ate at the dining room table. We had a radio and we would listen to cowboy shows and soap operas," she said.

Bryant's grandfather operated his own store, the Mathews Grocery, on the side of his home. The grocery sold essential items like bread, poultry, and milk, and during the summer months frozen fruit drinks known as Snowballs.

Bryant remembers her grandparents offering assistance to many families who had trouble covering their grocery bills. "There were a lot of people who couldn't afford to pay and my grandfather let people have credit... I remember my grandmother used to feed a lot of people when they didn't have any food. They would just come by the house and she would feed them," she said.

Bryant's grandfather also told stories nightly about his experiences as a slave. She said he worked for a family who later gave him a sizable amount of real estate for his services. "My grandfather saved his mistress from the Red men. He was a slave who worked in the house and when (the slaves) were freed, he saved his mistress.

"When he was freed, his mistress gave him two blocks (of property) on Belleville Street, the house on Newton Street and property in Mississippi. Because of his limited education and because they didn't have the money to pay the taxes on the property, he lost it all except for home on Newton Street," she said.

The neighborhood where Bryant and her family lived was integrated. She recalled that race relations were pleasant and tension rarely existed. "Our neighborhood was integrated. We never had a problem with race. We played with the whites in our neighborhood. It never phased us. We had to go to separate places, we knew that, but otherwise we got along," she said.

Like many African American women and young girls in Algiers, Bryant also worked as a domestic. She remembered domestic work as being the first job she had in her youth. "At that time things were real rough. You did what they called 'day's work.' I would go once or twice per week (to clean homes)," she said.

Children were also required to help with household chores that included gathering wood to be used at the home.

Wood was a precious commodity as it was used most commonly for wood-burning stoves. "We had to go to the SP (Southern Pacific Railroad) tracks under the Algiers Viaduct to pick up wood. There would be many of us out there with our carts to pick up wood. Sometimes we had to go in the morning before school started and after school," she said.

The Algiers Viaduct on Newton Street allowed citizens to cross the railroad tracks that separated the community. The Viaduct was constructed in 1907 for horsedrawn traffic and was later used for vehicular, street car and pedestrian travel.

Bryant's family attended St. John African Methodist Episcopal Church of Algiers located at 1017 Belleville Street. Like many churches in Algiers, youth activities were abundant. Bryant remembered taking lots of trips to visit other AME churches and attending church conventions.

"Being a Methodist, we visited other churches. We had a youth division. We had a baseball team and we would play other churches. The church often gave bus rides and there were church conferences at other churches in the (rural areas). In order for us to go on bus rides, we would have to raise our bus fare.

"It was usually about 50 cents. So we would collect soda bottles near the SP tracks and take them to the grocery store across the street from McDonogh #32 School. If we raised the bus fare, then our parents would buy our food for the trip. We would usually get a big loaf of bread and half luncheon meat and half cheese; and a bottle of soda," she said.

Bryant, like other residents, said that Algiers was a small and personable community. "The neighbors were very close. You could leave your doors unlocked. It was really good at that time. Everybody was together." Of the Depression she said, "We weathered the storm. That's the way you look at it. We've had some rough times and we survived through it."

Martha B. Mallory
Retired Business Manager

Martha B. Mallory poses for a photograph as a child in the early 1930s.

Martha B. Mallory was born in 1930 at the onset of the Depression. Her father died when she was one-year-old. Mallory's mother, Beatrice Mallory, worked as a domestic for Mary Vaugn of Algiers who was Principal of Adolph Meyer Elementary School.

Mallory recalled that several families in Algiers were poor yet willing to help others. "During my time of upbringing, nobody really had a lot, but what people did have, they didn't mind sharing. Families were closely knit, people were more compassionate then," she said.

Martha B. Mallory was the first Queen of L. B. Landry School in the late 1930s. She is shown here with members of the Royal Court.

Rebecca Conley, Martha B. Mallory's grandmother is shown here in 1931 at her home in Algiers.

Rebecca Conley feeds her grandaughter, Martha B. Mallory, at her home in Algiers in 1932.

Martha B. Mallory's cousins sit on the steps of a home in Algiers. The historic dwelling had storm doors that were an architectural standard for homes in the neighborhood.

Mallory attended the traditional neighborhood schools for African Americans, McDonogh #32 Elementary School and L.B. Landry School. Landry was an elementary school when it was first constructed in 1938 and gradually integrated high school grades at the urging of its principal, Israel M. Augustine and influental ministers in the community. Mallory also aftened All Saints Catholic School, Xavier Prepatory School and Xavier University. All of the schools' populations were and remain today, predominantly African American.

As a child, Mallory and her mother lived in a modest home in Algiers, but spent many days and nights at the Vaughn home at 229 Bermuda Street.

Vaughn employed a chauffer who would drive her to Adolph Meyer and then drive Mallory to school. Though the Mallory family enjoyed the luxuries and conveniences that living with Vaughn provided, the appearance of affluence caused some trouble for Mallory at school. "Children were cruel," she said. Being teased and called names because of her chauffer driven travel had become common for Mallory which led her mother to send her to another school.

Mallory remembered suffering scorn among whites in the community as well. "They would say, here comes Mary Vaughn and her niggers," she said as she recalled public outings where she, her mother and the chauffer would accompany Vaughn.

She said that there were other incidents that occurred in the neighborhood where Vaughn lived. "(One day) I left the house to go to the store. I passed a house and a lady was in her yard with her son. And she said, 'now you see son, that is a nigger.' I went on to the store and came back (to the house) and told May May (Mary Vaughn). And she went and confronted the lady about it... We didn't have no more trouble after that," she said.

Except for those isolated incidents, Mallory reported that race relations in Algiers were relatively good. "Segregation always existed," she said, "but most of the whites and blacks got along. We lived side by side, we were in and out of each other's houses, and the children played together."

Church activity during Mallory's youth was a large part of her formative years. "As children, we had Vacation Bible School. Our whole summer was utilized going to Vacation Bible School. Just about every church in Algiers had Vacation Bible School," she said. Mallory said her involvement in church activities began with youth ministries. She taught Sunday School, played the organ and participated in several church programs.

She studied music as a child and learned to play the piano and the violin. Her music teacher, Manual Manetta, was popular in Algiers and had taught several budding musicians in the community.

Second Good Hope Baptist Church, 800 Elmira Avenue.

The Reverend Webster Carroll, Pastor of Second Good Hope Baptist Church is surrounded by members of the Usher Board.

Two members of Second Good Hope Baptist Church stand near their chartered bus before boarding. Church picnics were popular in Algiers in the 1930s and 1940s.

Since the church played a central role in community life, Mallory said high moral standards were instilled in children continuously. "We had to have morals. It was taught to you day and night. And not only at home, but in school. At that time if students weren't doing right (in school), the teachers would call your parents. And parents didn't say, 'well my child said...' If the teacher said you did it, then the parent would say, 'I'll take care of it.' And we didn't have the telephones with (call waiting), but the news got home before you got there," she said.

Mallory said respect for elders was also high on the list of things to do for youth in Algiers. "One thing we had to do was, we had to respect older people."

"We had to say, 'good morning' and 'good evening' (as we passed others on the street). We had to go to school everyday. We couldn't say I don't want to go. We had a truant officer whose name was Ms. Azamore. She would come to your house and get you if you didn't come to school," she said.

Social clubs, carnival clubs, benevolent societies and church auxiliaries were also a mainstay in the Algiers community. Most of the groups provided services to its members and reached out into the community through charity events and fundraisers.

Mallory recalled that most of the societies had juvenile chapters that helped to develop young people into responsible citizens.

Several of the organizations have been disbanded because many of the older members have died. Benevolent societies phased out as insurance companies began offering policies that covered burial expenses that the organizations often provided to its members.

Some of the oldest and still active organizations include the Order of Eastern Star and the Prince Hall Masons' Pride of Algiers Lodge #102. Ladies of Perserverance is another service organization that is now about 94 years old and has close to 77 members.

Social activities for youth included dances at All Saints Catholic Church on Monday nights. Mallory remembered those days as fun times for all. "At that time you could walk the streets at night and nobody would bother you. We would go to the ice cream parlor and the Folly Theatre on Teche Street. As children we liked to ride bikes, play hopscotch, jax, jump rope and sometimes even play church... We invented the skooter. We would take an old skate and nail a piece of plywood on to it and ride," she said.

With poverty and small pockets of racisim surrounding them, the Mallory family made the most of their circumstances. Working for an affluent woman who had a generous spirit offered them perks and privledges that others were not privy to receive. "Basically, we didn't have it as bad as some," said Mallory.

The Great Depression was difficult for many, but like other African Americans who lived in Algiers, Mallory recalled a simple time where compassion overshadowed gloomy situations. "It was a good life, because right now I meet people that I was in school with and it's like we never parted... People were more concerned about each other," she said.

Beatrice Mallory (Martha B. Mallory's mother), the Reverend Webster Carroll and his wife Hilda Carroll.

Minerva Victor Simmons
Retired Civilian Employee, U.S. Navy

Minverva Victor Simmons was born in 1931 in the midst of the Great Depression. She remembered that her family was poor, yet capable of providing the basic neccessities such as food, clothing and shelter.

Simmons attended school at St. John African Methodist Episcipol Church, 1017 Belleville Street. The church was rented by the New Orleans Public School System to house kindergarten and first grade classes that the McDonogh #32 School, established in 1907, was incapable of accommodating. She received her junior high and high school education at L. B. Landry School, 1200 Whitney Avenue.

Landry was established in 1938 as an elementary school named for the late Dr. Lord Beaconsfield Landry, a prominent physician of the Algiers community. Through the urging of concerned community members, high school classes were added to Landry in 1939 and the school saw its first graduating class in 1943. Simmons remembered that those influential community members included the school's principal Israel M. Augustine, Sr., the Reverend Linden Herman Keiffer, the Reverend General Benjamin Franklin, Mrs. Viola Smith, the Reverend Arthur Monday, the Reverend James Lewis, the Reverend Charlie Williams, the Reverend Charles Harrison and several others.

Minerva Victor Simmons' father Albert Victor is pictured in the middle surrounded by Thelma Fortier Harrison and Leona Baxter. All three were first cousins.

The group was also successful in securing bus transporation for African American students in Algiers. Simmons graduated in Landry's second graduating class on June 2, 1948.

A newspaper clipping announcing Alex Ledet's retirement. Ledet was Minvera Simmons' grandmother's father making him her Great grandfather.

The eldest of eight children, Simmons' family lived in what was known as the Oakdale community of Algiers. The area was commonly known for a dairy farm that included large cow pastures, the now defunct New Salem Baptist Church and a bakery. Oakdale's current location is the area along Whitney Avenue where the Fischer Housing Development now stands.

Additionally, the existing neutral ground was formerly a canal that ran through Algiers. Simmons recalled that during her youth, many families that lived in Oakdale did not enjoy the conveniences of a sewerage system. Therefore, without indoor plumbing, the families were forced to use "out houses" and cisterns to collect water for drinking, bathing, cooking and cleaning.

Charles Ned, Simmons' stepgrandfather and her grandmother's second husband.

Minerva Ledet Victor Ned (Simmons' grandmother) and Retta Mae Ledet Robinson (her grandmother's niece).

Simmons said the biggest fear that community members shared was stepping on a snake en route to the out house. "We didn't have to worry about people killing us back then, we had to worry about stepping on a snake going to the out house," she said.

Cold winters and hot summers were also the normal conditions of life in Algiers during Simmons' youth. To cool off during the hot summer months was a challenge she said and although some homes had fans, many did not. "You had to open the windows in the summer for air and those who were well off had screens on the windows. Some people had fans, but not many. We didn't have any. We had to fold up newspapers and fan with that. Some people used to put nets over their beds to keep out musquitos, but not many had that either," she said.

Simmons' mother, now in her 90s, dropped out of school in the third grade and began work as a domestic to assist her family. Simmons also worked as a domestic during summer vacations beginning in her eighth-grade year of school. She remembered that several young women held domestic jobs during the summer cleaning homes and caring for babies in the homes of Algiers' white residents.

Simmons said she and her peers were sometimes ashamed to let others know that they worked in the homes of whites and would often avoid neighborhood excursions with white babies to avoid the eyes of their friends.

These photographs are contained in Simmons' family album. The names of these Algiers men are unknown, but date back to World War I.

She remembered that her sister once told a male admirer that she was a clerk for an affluent white family rather than a domestic. When the young gentleman discovered the truth, her sister was laughed at and teased for years.

Today, however, Simmons and her family laugh at their perceptions of performing such work as they have now come to realize that many African Americans that provided domestic services used the profession as a means to educate themselves and their children so that future generations would not have to do such work.

Men in the Algiers community held jobs at the Southern Pacific Railroad, the dry docks and some became merchant seamen. In addition to manual labor jobs, farming or "gardening" was popular in Algiers during the Depression.

Simmons recalled that her grandfather leased portions of undeveloped land to grow crops. "He would plow land for the corn, tomatoes, beans, crowder peas or cow peas,"she said. These crops would yield a considerable amount of vegetables that contributed greatly to the family's food supply. Meat and other products for cooking was purchased at local grocery stores.

Simmons remembered that November was "hog killing" season and neighborhood residents looked forward to the event. "My grandfather had a wagon to get slop for the hogs and in November, when it was cold, he would kill a hog. He would then dig a hole in the ground and take a rack and put it over the hole.

*The Reverend Linden Herman Keiffer was a close friend of Charles Ned,
Simmons' stepgrandfather. Keiffer was also the Pastor of Mt. Sinai Baptist
Church of Algiers.*

"Then he would take seasonings like garlic, onions and celery, and put it in the hole. He would put the hog on the rack over a slow fire and start cooking it on a Friday night. The hog wouldn't be done until the next day. And while it was cooking, he would use a small mop to baste the hog in sauce... We would make cracklin' out of the hog skin and fry some sweet potatoes and sprinkle sugar on it for dessert. We would scrape all the fat off the hog intestines and then clean them and that would be used for the casing for blood sausage and boudin. We would also pickle the pig's feet, tail, lip, ears and so on. We didn't throw nothing away on the hog," she said.

Simmons remembered that after a hog was killed, cooked and pickled, parts were distributed liberally to community members, as people often shared food with each other.

Entertainment in the community could always be found at churches and schools. Christmas and Easter plays and Operettas were most commonly held at local churches or L.B. Landry School.

Football games and other sporting events were also frequented by community members and held at a local park named for one of its citizens.

"We would go to Landry football games at Risby Park and back then (Landry) didn't have a band, we had a letter squad that would go out on the field and form the letters LBL... I wanted to be in everything and sometimes my mother would tell me that we couldn't afford it and I would go to my grandfather and grandmother (for the money)," she said.

Simmons remembered her life in Algiers with great fondness and spoke light-heartedly about her living conditions even though it was obvious that times were hard. She admits that there were many things about those times that she does not want to remember. However, like other residents of the community, she too recalled that life was simple and void of many material possessions, but full of love, kindness and concern for others.

Minerva's family member.

Leaving Home

American History, by by Richard N. Current, Harry Williams, Frank Freidel and Alan Brinkley, recounts that African Americans experienced devastating hardships in the 1930s. Homelessness, malnutrition and disease was experienced to a far greater degree than in the past. Additionally, many African American farmers were left with no income at all when the prices for cotton and other staple crops collapsed. This forced several thousands of African Americans to leave the rural South and go north for better opportunities. This mass migration altered the lives of individuals and communities.

Many Algiers residents have family members who joined the ranks of those that left the South for a better life. Some left their families and never returned. Others left, maintained their family ties, but were unable to visit home often because of limited financial resources. Minerva Simmons recalled that one her relatives left New Orleans for Chicago and eventually died having never visited home again. Years later, though, her relative's daughter was able to visit the family and reported that her mother often talked about what life was like in Algiers. In addition to Chicago, other places that Algierines migrated to included New York and California.

Band Director William Houston directs the L.B. Landry High School Band in the late 1940s.

McDonogh #32 Elementary School students ride on a float during an annual parade hosted by the school in the 1940s.

Three students of L.B. Landry High School sit for a photo at the school's entrance in the late 1940s

Members of the girl's basketball team at L.B. Landry High School played competively as shown in the photo taken in the late 1940s

L.B. Landry High School (1940s) is shown in the background of this photo taken at a nearby pool used for recreation by students.

Three L.B. Landry Majorettes get ready for a football game to be held at Risby Park sometime in the late 1940s.

L.B. Landry High
School's football team
was known throughout
the City of New Orleans.
Two team members
posed for this photo in the
1940s.

The men's basketball
team at L.B. Landry
High School was among
the best. This photo was
taken in the late 1949s.

It was reported that in the 1930s, more than 400,000 African Americans left the South. Family ties, strong communities and limited financial resources lulled others into staying. However, the migration never ceased and Algiers lost hundreds of its African American citizens throughout the 1940s, the 1950s, the 1960s and even up until today.

The main reason for leaving was and still is the pursuit of better economic opportunities and a fair chance to obtain a job based on skills rather than skin color. Though many have left, some still remain and even more come home often to visit. It is not uncommon to meet or talk to Algiers residents who have family members that live either in New York, California, Washington, Chicago and other cities in the North or the West.

Most recently migrants have returned to Southern cities that include Georgia, Texas, Florida and Mississippi. However, all reside in those cities because economic opportunities are far more abundant.

The ages of those who live in other cities vary as some older residents have returned home after finishing their careers. Yet, the lack of jobs and fair opportunities drove many African Americans who hailed from Algiers to the North in search of a better life. The majority of those residents who remained in the community worked as educators, laborers, domestics and small business owners.

It almost never snows in New Orleans, except for this unexpected day in the 1950s. These homes are located in the Oakdale community of Algiers.

Manual P. Lombard's Ice, Coal and Wood Shop sponsored a baseball team in the late 1940s. Team members paused for a photo at practice.

Beautiful Zion Baptist Church was established in 1871. Pictured is the Church's choir with its Pastor, Reverend H.J. Gilliam.

The Senior Usher Board.

The Beautiful Zion Baptist Church Sunday School gathered for a class photo in the 1950s.

The Sunday School is pictured in 1966.

Moses and Gloria Bailey were high school sweathearts when they posed for these photographs in the 1940s.

Frances Granderson, Ernestine Cosey and Gloria Bailey are pictured at Granderson's home in the Oakdale community of Algiers.

Frances Granderson is pictured at her 100th Birthday Celebration at Mt. Sinai Baptist Church.

First Free Mission Baptist Church, established in the 1800s, is the oldest African American church in Algiers.

Social club functions such as balls and dances were common in Algiers. Young socialites are pictured at the Gay Jesters Ball in the 1950s.

Beautiful Zion Baptist Church members at its old facility in the 1950s. The church began its services here in 1917.

Beautiful Zion Baptist Church members gather for a photo in 1966.

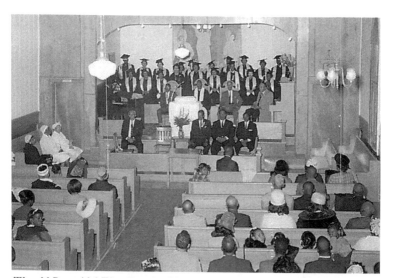

The old Beautiful Zion Baptist Church pictured was demolished in 1965.

The new Beautiful Zion Baptist Church pictured was completed in 1966.

Chapter Two
World War II and After

The history of African Americans serving in the armed forces is a history that is rich and can be traced to such conflicts as the American Revolution and Civil War. As the tradition of joining the armed forces among African Americans was common, so was their belief that social and economic conditions would improve for them as a result of their service. Unfortunately, all too often, they were cruelly disappointed.

This disappointment is evidenced by the segregated conditions in America that welcomed African Americans after their service in World War I. Many were told that their service abroad would help to improve race relations, and social and economic conditions at home. This was untrue and as World War II was declared, many African Americans had to be drafted in order to be counted among those willing to risk their lives for the nation. Young men between the ages of 18 and 45 were drafted from Algiers and, like many World War II Veterans, recall incidences of racial segregation in foreign countries as well as at home.

Nicholas Jefferson was one of many Algiers men who served in the Armed Forces during the War. This photo was taken in the 1940s.

Reverend Forest, Associate Minister at Mt. Pilgrim Fourth Baptist Church served in World War II. The photo dates back to the early 1940s.

John R. Spencer was drafted into the United States Navy and served in World War II. This photo dates back to the early 1940s.

World War II Veteran Philip Watson, Sr. served in the United States Army. This photo was taken sometime in the 1940s.

Herbert Simpson

Veteran, Former Pro Baseball Player

Herbert "Briefcase" Simpson was known for his line drives that secured base hits in the heat of the game. He is shown here as a Harlem Globetrotter team member in 1947.

Herbert Simpson, originally from Hahnville, Louisiana, grew up in Algiers at 1212 Brooklyn Street. As a young boy, he played baseball in the neighborhood with his playmates. His father, Horace Simpson, who played baseball with the Negro Leagues, taught him to play the game.

Simpson remembered that it was Alex Winnfield's team that gave him his start as a baseball player at nine-years-old. He recalled playing three or four innings at Algiers Giants' games. The Algiers Giants team consisted of adult players that competed against other African American baseball teams.

Simpson continued to play ball during his adolescent years and word of his talent began to spread. In the early 1940s, after graduating high school, he was recruited by Wesley Barrow and Winfield Welch to join the Birmingham Black Barons, a professional team of the Negro Baseball League. Simpson played first base and outfield.

He was known for his line drives that made him a reliable player in securing base hits during crucial moments of the game.

Simpson was slowly making a name for himself in professional baseball and earned the name Herb "Briefcase" Simpson. However, his career was soon interrupted in 1942, when he was drafted into the United States Army. After several months in training camp, where incidently he continued to play baseball, Simpson traveled abroad to continue his military service. He spent a total of three years in the military during the War.

Two years were spent in England, and six months each in France and Germany. Simpson recalled that his military unit, Company 2057, never participated in direct combat, but provided weapons to the men who fought on the front line.

Simpson remembered a day when a "bomb dump" (storage site) exploded only minutes after his Company had left. "We got out (of the bomb dump) one day and the dump blew up. And they said, 'wow how lucky can those guys be,'" he said.

In addition to risking their lives at the bomb dump, Simpson's Company also had to dodge bullets and run when carrying weapons to and from the heat of battle. He said bombing was common and remembered a bomb that once exploded a mere block away from their location.

Added to all the near-death experiences that Simpson and his Company experienced were the incidences of racial segregation. Though his Company was made up of African Americans, the Commanding Officer was white. Also, many restaurants and nightclubs in England and France were off-limits to African Americans.

When D-Day arrived, Simpson's Company was relieved of their duties on the front line. Later they discovered that many of the men that they had carried weapons to, lost their lives. They were fortunate to not be among the dead. "... they killed them all. My Commanding Officer told me, 'you don't drink, but you will today. They told us they don't want us and we don't want to go. Let's go get drunk.' I didn't drink so one of the other soldiers drank my beer," he said.

Simpson spent the latter part of his military service in Germany where he said the stench from dead bodies was sickening. He recalled mass graves or trenches where bodies where dumped and buried. He also remembered passing concentration camps where he saw horrific scenes of death and deterioration. "I didn't like to pass those things. We would pass the concentration camps and the people would be so skinny they looked like skin and bones, and their hair was so long. I don't know what was keeping them alive," he said.

Simpson was discharged in 1946 and remembered his homecoming as a joyful time for his family. "I had called my parents and told them I was coming home. When I got home and got to the ferry, a guy told me not to catch a cab. He said I might be brought somewhere and robbed because they may think that I have money.

"So I caught the bus. It was about ten cents then, and I got off on Diana Street. I was living in the 1200 block on Brooklyn Street behind (Murray) Henderson Funeral Home. I rang the bell and my sister Claudette came to open the door and said, 'mama, they have a policeman at the door.' My mama said, 'A policeman don't have no business at this door.' My daddy came to the door and he said, 'that's no policeman, that's my boy!'

"My mama was so excited. And my daddy grabbed me and kissed me, and my mama kissed me. I couldn't go to sleep that night. They asked me more questions and different things. My grandmother was living a few doors down and

Herbert Simpson is pictured with the Harlem Globetrotters in 1948 (first row, second from right).

Another Harlem Globetrotters team photo depicts Simpson at the beginning of his career (first from right).

they called her and told her I was home. She said, 'ask him what he feels like eating. I told her I wanted some file' gumbo and I ate and it was some good. Everybody that came along asked me so many questions... I answered what I could. I went to church that Sunday morning and everybody was so glad to see me. I wouldn't want to go back into the service though. They didn't treat the Negroes like they should have," he said.

Shortly after Simpson and several other servicemen were discharged from the military, he was offered a job playing professional baseball. Simpson said other young men from Algiers were also offered jobs in pro baseball. They included Dave Celestine, J.B. Spencer, John Jackson, and Lucien Leonard.

Simpson began his professional career with the Seattle Steelheads in the Negro Pacific League. From there he played for the Cincinnati Crescents. While a player for the Crescents, Simpson traveled to Hawaii to play in an all-star game and track star Jesse Owens served as their business manger.

The team played 16 games and won 15 total. The following season, Simpson joined the Harlem Globetrotters where he played some of the greatest ball players in the history of the game. The Spokane Indians was the next team that Simpson played for before becoming the first African American to play for a team in Albuquerque, New Mexico.

He broke the color barrier in the West Texas-New Mexico League as a team member of the Albuquerque AA Dukes. It was during his career with the team in Albuquerque that Simpson married his longtime love at home plate. The entire ceremony was publicized and paid for by his team. Simpson's family traveled to New Mexico for the wedding and his new bride stayed with him an additional week before returning to New Orleans.

Months later, Simpson ended his baseball career and returned to New Orleans. He worked for the Johns-Mansville plant, the New Orleans Public Schools and the State of Louisiana before retiring.

Tyrone Casby, Sr.

Principal, McDonogh #32 Elementary School

Tyrone Casby, Sr. is a sixth generation Casby family member.

Tyrone Casby, Sr. was born in Algiers and comes from a family with deep roots in the community. His uncle owned a shoe repair store in the community and several of his family members were known for their strong work ethics.

Casby's grandfather, William Casby was 14-years-old when Algiers was annexed to the City of New Orleans in 1870 and lived to be 114-years old before his death.

Tyrone is a sixth generation Casby and still lives and works in the community that he calls home. Though he was born in 1953, well after World War II, Casby remembered many stories told to him as a youth by his grandfather and uncles. He said that after the War had ended, African Americans in Algiers began to demand more social and economic benefits that had been previously denied them because of their race. A major issue was the lack of fair job opportunities as some positions were off-limits to African Americans.

Casby remembered that War Veterans in Algiers began to seek positions with agencies such as the United States Post Office. Additionally, Veteran status provided many community members with the means to purchase homes. Truman Park, a small subdivision in the Oakdale community of Algiers, was constructed in the 1950s as a result of efforts initiated after the War.

Casby's uncles also told him stories of the harsh segregation that African American soldiers endured in the War. It had become common knowledge among community members in Algiers that the men were mistreated and not afforded the same rights as white soldiers during World War II.

Just as African American men throughout the United States felt the sting of serving a country that considered them second-class citizens, the men of Algiers who served, shared those sentiments.

It was the postwar disposition of African Americans throughout America that gave rise to the Civil Rights Movement, and Algiers, though a small and isolated community, began to show small signs of change.

Tyrone Casby became active in the fight for Civil Rights at the age of 11-years-old. Many of his uncles were actively involved in petitioning the white community for increased social and economic benefits and Casby was taken in as a prodigy.

Tyrone Casby, Sr. is pictured at left with his family. The Casby family has been a part of Algiers since it was annexed to the City of New Orleans in 1870.

Tyrone Casby, Sr. (right), his son (left), grandson (front) and his daughter (below).

As Big Chief of the Mohawk Hunters Mardi Gras Indian Tribe, Tyrone Casby, Sr. and his family produce beautiful costumes each year in honor of this New Orleans tradition. The Mohawk Hunters have participated in parades as early as 1943. The group was organized in the Oakdale community of Algiers. Photo: The Times-Picayune, 2011

"I became involved in civil rights after World War II," he said, "(African American men) had endured so much during the War that they wanted to make a difference when they came home," he said.

Casby came from a family of 15 brothers and sisters, of which he was the middle child. Following his uncles' lead came natural and Casby participated in Civil Rights marches, joined a youth group that provided social services to the less fortunate and became an all-around social and civil activist.

Another Algiers resident who became active in the Civil Rights struggle is Lula Mae B. Ward. Ward remembered that the desire for fair treatment in society was great, but change in Algiers was slow and eventually had to be forced.

Ward was raised at 411 DeArmas Street. Her parents, Lillian and Philip Watson, had five children and raised their children with strong moral convictions. Philip Watson served in World War II, as did many men in Algiers. He, too, longed for the day when better jobs would be available to him.

Ward remembered that her father worked on the dry docks and was forced to share his earnings with white men who helped him secure the position.

Ward also remembered that many African Americans could not purchase their own homes. It was not until 1955 when a developer visited Beautiful Zion Baptist Church and held an informal seminar that African Americans began accomplishing their goals of home ownership. "We had jobs, we had bank accounts, but we couldn't buy our own homes," she said.

In addition to housing discrimination, African Americans in Algiers were also subjected to Jim Crow laws that were prevalent throughout the South. When traveling by bus or by streetcar, African Americans sat behind screens.

The screens were mobile and could be moved further back during bus travel to accommodate whites who needed seats on the bus. Therefore, African Americans would be forced to move as the screen moved.

Public places such as restaurants were off-limits to African Americans in Algiers. Several residents reported that if an African American person chose to go to a neighborhood restaurant or eatery, they would have to order from the back door or a side window.

White doctors in Algiers also enforced similar restrictions. There were many doctors, however, who treated African American patients after normal business hours or made house calls. Dr. LaRocca and Dr. Ernest Schiro, white physicians, and Dr. Calderonne, a white pharmacist, are beloved to this day because of their commitment and service to the African American community in spite of the laws of segregation.

Entertainment for African Americans in Algiers was limited to church activities, school functions and segregated night spots. The Folly Theater was reserved for African

American patrons as they were not allowed in the Avalon Theater on Opelousas Street. Certain areas of Algiers were also off-limits to African Americans, not by law, but by intimidation. Older residents remembered that unless an African American person was working in the neighborhoods beginning at Opelousas and ending at the river, the area was otherwise off-limits to them.

Shopping also proved to be a challenge for African Americans living in Algiers. Many said that rather than endure the shame of venturing into department stores, they sewed their own clothes. Canal Street, the heart of the business and retail market in New Orleans, was not a welcoming place for many African Americans.

Minerva Simmons and others remembered trying on clothes in stock rooms of department stores. In some cases, African Americans were not allowed to try on garments at all. Department store credit was not an option for African Americans who were often forced to pay for items using a monthly payment plan called "lay away."

Simmons, who worked for a major department store early in her career, recalled that white customers did not want African Americans serving them in the stores. She also remembered that African American customers were assigned secret codes that often contributed to a merchant's decision to deny them store credit. "It took a black person 10 days to qualify for credit and a white person 10 minutes," she said.

Segregation was a normal and, unfortunately, accepted way of life. In Algiers, segregation prevented the races from interacting publicly and relegated African Americans to subservient positions in society.

The Algiers neighborhoods, however, were sometimes different from the larger community. Though the laws mandated separation, Algiers residents interacted often with whites in their neighborhoods.

"I remember playing with white children, but I couldn't sit at their dinner table. They could sit at mine, but I couldn't sit at theirs.

"Also, we didn't go to school with them, but we treated each other as if we were sisters and brothers," said Tyrone Casby.

Almost all African American Algiers residents recalled that race relations in the community were pleasant. Neighbors treated one another with kindness and respect.

Very often, African Americans lived in mixed neighborhoods and to have a white neighbor was common. Racial integration had been achieved in the neighborhoods, but integrating schools and public facilities took longer. In 1955, Brown vs. the Board of Education of Topeka, Kansas declared that separate but equal laws were unjust and that public schools must be integrated.

Public schools in Algiers and the City of New Orleans would eventually integrate, according to the law, marking the beginning of the end to an important period in the history of Algiers' African American community.

Epilogue

It is said that the good and the bad shall dwell together in the world. In small communities like Algiers, the principle holds true. As all human experiences reveal, life is made up of mountains and valleys.

It is obvious that African Americans in the United States have been in more valleys than on mountains. However, the African Americans that lived in Algiers said that although they dwelled in the valley, their faith in God and strong cultural traditions helped to help them make it to the mountain.

With a heritage that was rooted on slave plantations and in servitude, it would seem like their futures were destined to be full of hopelessness. Material wealth did not exist for African Americans living in Algiers, and poverty was so common that many people said that they were poor, but didn't know it. Poverty was the norm and people did what they had to do to survive.

Algiers was a place where neighbors of all races cared for each other. They shared their talents, food, clothing and whatever they could to help someone in need.

It was a place where faith in God was the source of all strength. Almost everyone belonged to a church in the community and they faithfully attended services and community programs sponsored by churches.

Moral values were instilled in African Americans as young children who were taught to apply the principles of the Bible to their everyday lives. Being kind and polite were top priorities for children and adults alike.

"Love thy neighbor as thyself" was preached in the pulpit on Sunday and practiced in the neighborhoods throughout the week. Crime and theft did not haunt the Algiers community of old as many residents said that doors could be left unlocked for days at a time without one item being touched or destroyed. The ministers in the Algiers community were social activists. They provided moral and spiritual guidance, cared for the sick, assisted the less fortunate, provided transportation, served as public advocates and fought for the rights of African American citizens in Algiers. Many of the social, political and economic gains that were achieved in the community were initiated by the African American ministers.

Education was another top priority for African Americans living in Algiers. They were often denied the right to receive the same quality of education as their white counterparts, but they still yearned for the opportunity to advance their positions in society. One African American woman who grew up in Algiers said that in her home, God was first, the family was second and getting an education was third. African Americans knew the power of having a quality education, and they believed that it would unlock the doors of opportunity for generations to follow.

The cultural traditions in the African American community in Algiers were strong and rich. Not only did they contain African traditions, but they were mixed with the cultural influences of the French and the Caribbean.

Though annexed to New Orleans in the 1800s, Algiers still maintained its own identity and social norms. Life was different on the Westbank of New Orleans. Small community values were held in high regard. Those values tied community members to one another. Those values inspired even the poor to care for those who were poorer. Those values shaped the lives of their children and transformed them into traditions that are still practiced today.

The good and the bad shall dwell together in this world, and the same holds true for the citizens of Algiers. The difference is, that the people chose to cling to all that is good and perfect to help them weather the storm, make it through the valley and reach the mountain.

Lagniappe

Felix James, also known as Coach James, is a beloved son of the Algiers community. Though he was not a native, he worked at L.B. Landry High School as a teacher and head coach of the football, basketball and track teams in the 1950s. James was instrumental in ensuring that several Algiers athletes have the opportunity to attend college. James' coaching accolades include local, state and national titles. He is a community figure that is well-spoken of and honored for his commitment to helping young people succeed.

Alvin Aubry is another honorary member of the Algiers community by way of L.B. Landry High School. Aubry is known for his stern discipline and his quest to provide Algiers youth with outstanding educational experiences. In a recent interview he said, "Throughout my stay, all professional leaders, mothers, fathers and ministers supported the school. They contributed to the success of the school." Aubry is highly regarded and his contributions are still appreciated by many community members.

Councilman *Troy Carter* is Algiers' first African American State Representative and City Councilman. His family ties to Algiers are deep and he continues to support the area through business and other economic pursuits.

Important Institutions in Algiers 1929–1955

African American Schools

- All Saints Catholic School
- L.B. Landry Junior / Senior High School
- McDonogh #5 School
- McDonogh #32 Elementary School
- St. John African Methodist Episcopal Church
- African American Churches
- All Saints Catholic Church

African American Churches

- First Free Mission Baptist Church
- Greater Morning Star Baptist Church
- Greater Providence Baptist Church
- Mt. Olive Baptist Church
- Mt. Pilgrim Fourth Baptist Church
- Mt. Sinai Baptist Church
- New Salem Baptist Church
- Olive Branch Baptist Church
- Second Good Hope Baptist Church
- Shiloh Baptist Church

- St. John AME Church
- St. Joseph Baptist Church
- St. Mark Baptist Church
- St. Mathew United Methodist Church
- St. Stephens Baptist Church
- Sunrise Baptist Church

African American & White Owned Businesses

- Avalon Theatre
- Barnes Shoe Shine Parlor
- Breaux's Seafood
- Ms. Sarah Brown - Midwife Services
- Buck's Famous Fried Chicken
- Dr. Caledronne's Pharmacy
- Campbell's Beer Parlor
- V. Centineo's Grocery Store
- Chifici's Grocery Store
- Corona's Food Store
- Simon Craig Dry Cleaners
- Damico's - Blacksmith
- Dolcich & Rovira - Electronic Specialists
- Bernice Durden Franklin's School of Dancing
- Fager's Drug Store
- Ella's Fried Chicken and Fish
- Elks Hall

- Fitzgerald Florist
- Folly Theatre
- Gendusa's Grocery Store
- W.T. Goodwynne Grocery Store
- Greystone Lounge
- Gilbert's Barber Shop
- Julia Hadley - Herbal Doctor
- Mrs. L. B. Hill - Beautician
- Wesley Hill - Insurance Salesman
- Hooper's Cash Grocery Store
- Household Appliance Company
- Johnny's Grocery
- Philip Jones - Ice Box Maker
- King Kotton Shoppe
- Kolhman's Cab Service
- Lamothe Grocery Store
- Dr. Henry A. La Rocca
- LaSalle-Gilbert Drug Store
- Manual P. Lombard - Wood, Ice & Coal Shop
- Leon Lombard - Wood, Ice & Coal Shop
- Louis Ice Cream Parlor
- Marshall Cabs
- Masonic Temple

- Mott's
- T&T Notion Store and Cab Service
- Patai Radio Sales and Service
- Big Red's Filling Station
- Red's Bicycle Shop
- Rosebud Refreshment Center
- Rantz Ice Factory
- Star Shoe Store
- Saleeby's Shoe Store
- Seven Sisters - Spiritualists
- George Splan - Ice Man
- Clarence Swayne - Bus Service
- Soulant Liquors
- Summerlin Restaurant
- Thelma's Beauty Shoppe
- A.W. Thompson, Piano Tuner
- Thomas Taylor Cab Service
- Viadcut Filling Station
- Vic's Liquor Store
- Weiner's Furniture Store
- Westside Casino Bar
- Westside Cleaners
- Holly Wilson's Barber Shop

- Weileman's Bakery

African American Organizations

- Algiers Giants Baseball Team
- Algiers Dr. Nut Joints Baseball Team
- American Legion, Nelson Harper Post 554
- Order of Eastern Star, Star Hope Chapter #17
- Elks 999 IBPOW
- Free Women in Christ
- Gay Jesters
- Girlfriends
- Household of Ruth #2029
- Jugs Social Aid & Pleasure Club / New Orleans Most Talked About Club(NOMTOC)
- Ladies of Perseverance
- Mohawk Hunters Indian Tribe
- Old Timers Baseball League
- Prince Hall Masons, Pride of Algiers Lodge #102
- Veterans of Foreign Wars #2403
- Westside Quarterback Club
- Westside Revelers Carnival Club
- Grand United Order of Odd Fellows

Small Communities in and around Algiers

- Cut Off
- Gretna
- Harvey
- Oakdale
- Marrero
- McDonoghville
- McCleadonville (some say McClineyville)
- Westwego

Structures of Old

- Newton Street Viaduct
- Algiers Canal
- Old Footbridge

References

- Current, Richard N.; Williams, T. Harry; Freidel, Frank; Brinkley, Alan, *American History: A Survey, Volume II: Since 1865* (Knopf, 1987).

- Meyer, Robert, Jr., *Names Over New Orleans Public Schools* (Namesake Press, 1975).

- DeVore, Donald E.; Logsdon, Joseph, *Crescent City Schools: Public Education in New Orleans, 1841-1991* (The Center for Louisiana Studies University of Southwestern Louisiana, 1991).

- Kelley, Brent, *The Negro Leagues Revisited* (McFarland, 2000).

- The Buccaneer Souvenir Program Book, L.B. Landry School, 1947.

- Dixon, Richard, *This Is Algiers* (Upton Printing, 1971).

- Dixon, Richard, Algiers: *The Centennial Year - 1970-71* (1972).

- Louisiana Weekly, November 1933.

- McNabb, Donald and Madere, Lee, *A History of New Orleans* (Lee Madere, 1997).

Photograph Credits

- Lillian Alveris Williams – pages 9, 11, 12, 13, 15, 17

- Erma Henderson Gibbs – page 23

- Martha B. Mallory – pages 31, 32, 33, 34, 36, 37, 40

- Minerva Victor Simmons – pages 42, 43, 44, 45, 47, 49, 51

- Gloria and Moses Bailey – pages 53, 54, 55, 56, 58

- Beautiful Zion Baptist Church – pages 59, 60, 61, 62, 63, 64, 65

- Lillian Watson – pages 67, 68

- Herbert Simpson – pages 69, 73

- Tyrone Casby, Sr. – pages 76, 79, 80

Made in the USA
Monee, IL
15 July 2024

61856182R00057